7/04

14.95

Ecosystems

Rain Forests

Greg Reid

CHELSEA
CLUBHOUSE

An Imprint of Chelsea House Publishers
A Haights Cross Communications Company
Philadelphia

To Mary-Anne, Julian and Damian

This edition first published in 2004 in the United States of America by Chelsea Clubhouse, a division of Chelsea House Publishers and a subsidiary of Haights Cross Communications.

Chelsea Clubhouse
1974 Sproul Road, Suite 400
Broomall, PA 19008-0914

The Chelsea House world wide web address is www.chelseahouse.com

Library of Congress Cataloging-in-Publication Data Applied for.

ISBN 0-7910-7941-4

First published in 2004 by
MACMILLAN EDUCATION AUSTRALIA PTY LTD
627 Chapel Street, South Yarra, Australia, 3141

Associated companies and representatives throughout the world.

Edited by Anna Fern and Miriana Dasovic
Text and cover design by Polar Design
Illustrations and maps by Alan Laver, Shelly Communications
Photo research by Legend Images

Printed in China

Acknowledgments

The author and publisher are grateful to the following for permission to reproduce copyright material:

Cover photograph: an ocelot in a rain forest understory, courtesy of Photolibrary.com/Animals Animals.

Tui De Roy/Auscape International, pp. 12, 19 (center right); Jacques Jangoux/Auscape International, p. 5 (bottom left); Kevi Schaffer – Peter Arnold/Auscape International, pp. 8, 23; Michael Sewell – Peter Arnold/Auscape International, p. 19 (center left); John Shaw/Auscape International, p. 9 (bottom); Australian Picture Library/Corbis, pp. 13 (bottom), 19 (bottom), 20, 27; Corbis Digital Stock, pp. 3 (top & bottom), 15 (both), 18 (bottom), 30 (left), 31; Digital Vision, pp. 13 (top right), 16 (top), 17 (both), 19 (top center); Getty Images/Taxi, p. 13 (center right); Hans & Judy Beste/Lochman Transparencies, p. 14; Brett Dennis/Lochman Transparencies, p. 10 (bottom); Jiri Lochman/Lochman Transparencies, pp. 5 (right), 9 (top), 18 (inset); Marie Lochman/Lochman Transparencies, p. 11 (inset); Jerry Callow/panos pictures, p. 11 (bottom); Fred Hoogervorst/panos pictures, p. 19 (top left); Pelusey Photography, pp. 7 (top right, bottom left & bottom right), 28; Photodisc, pp. 3 (center), 6, 7 (top left & bottom center), 24, 25 (both), 26, 30 (right), 32; Photolibrary.com/Animals Animals, p. 16 (bottom); Reuters, pp. 21, 29; The G.R. "Dick" Roberts Photo Library, pp. 13 (top left), 22.

Please note
At the time of printing, the Internet addresses appearing in this book were correct. Owing to the dynamic nature of the Internet, however, we cannot guarantee that all these addresses will remain correct.

The author would like to thank Anatta Abrahams, Janine Hanna, Eulalie O'Keefe, Kerry Regan, Marcia Reid.

Contents

When a word is printed in **bold**, you can look up its meaning in the Glossary on page 31.

What Are Rain Forests?

Rain forests are wet, green jungles that are full of life. A rain forest environment is part of an ecosystem. An ecosystem is made up of living plants and animals and their non-living environment of air, water, energy, and nutrients.

Rain forest trees crowd close together and act as highways for animal life. The trees are also covered with orchids and ferns. Vines climb the trunks and branches, fighting to reach the Sun. Palms, ferns, shrubs, and mosses grow underneath in the shadows.

Rain forests are home to millions of **species** of plants, insects, mammals, birds, reptiles, and other animals. Many of the rain forest species are **unique**. Scientists believe there are millions more types of plants and animals yet to be discovered.

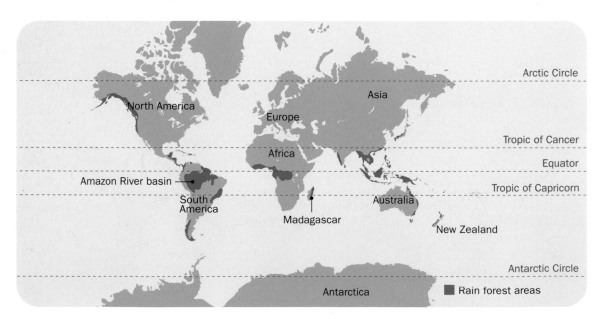

Most rain forests are found around the Equator, between the Tropic of Cancer and the Tropic of Capricorn. Rain forests in this region are called tropical rain forests. The weather here is always hot and wet.

Where Do Rain Forests Grow?

Rain forests grow in every continent except Antarctica and Europe. The Amazon River basin in South America has the largest area of rain forest. It covers an area of about 2 million square miles (5.2 million square kilometers).

Large areas of rain forest also grow across Central America and parts of Africa and southern Asia. Smaller areas of rain forest grow in Madagascar, Australia, and many islands in the Pacific Ocean. Brazil, Zaire, and Indonesia have more than half of the world's rain forests.

Where rain forests are found

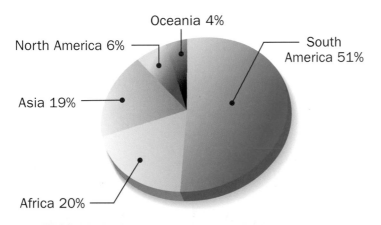

Oceania 4%

North America 6%

South America 51%

Asia 19%

Africa 20%

Shrinking Rain Forests

Once, rain forests covered about 15 percent of Earth's land surface. Today, they cover only about 7 percent because they have been cleared for timber and farming.

Rain forests in Madagascar have been destroyed by slash-and-burn farming.

The Amazon River and rain forest, in Brazil

Climate

Areas with rain forests have regular rainfall. Most rain forests receive at least 80 inches (2,000 millimetres) of rain a year and have high humidity. The air seems heavy and wet. Rainfall is usually spread evenly throughout the year. Dry spells are usually short.

Most rain forests grow in areas where temperatures range from 68 to 82 degrees Fahrenheit (20 to 28 degrees Celsius) year round. Near the Equator, the temperature varies by only a few degrees daily, and stays the same for most of the year. Farther away from the Equator, temperatures vary throughout the day and night. Some areas also have seasons, with warmer and cooler weather.

A tropical rainstorm

Daily Weather Cycle

Many rain forests near the Equator have a daily weather cycle. As the morning Sun heats up the land, the temperature and the humidity quickly rise. Clouds begin to build up and, by midday, they cover the sky. The clouds are full of moisture and, around 3 P.M., thunderstorms drop heavy rainfall. By 5 P.M., the storms have cleared, but the sky remains cloudy. Nights are cloudy, and the temperature and humidity go down only slightly.

Morning—clear sunny sky

Midday—complete cloud cover

The daily weather cycle

Night—some cloud cover

Mid-afternoon—thunderstorm

Late afternoon—cloudy

Types of Rain Forests

The climate, plants, and animals in a rain forest can vary by location and elevation, or height above sea level.

Tropical Rain Forests

The largest rain forests are the tropical rain forests. They cover only 6 percent of Earth's land. Tropical rain forests are hot and wet all year because they are close to the Equator. More than half of all the world's plants and animals live in tropical rain forests.

High-Elevation Rain Forests

Highland rain forests occur at heights above 3,300 feet (1,000 meters). They have fewer types of plants and animals compared with **lowland rain forests**.

Above 10,000 feet (3,000 meters), there are **cloud forests**. These forests are nearly always covered in clouds because they are so high.

Cloud forest in the Andes Mountains, Ecuador

Subtropical Rain Forests

These forests are found just outside the tropics. Temperatures here are slightly cooler, but these areas still receive a lot of rain. Subtropical rain forests have fewer types of plants and animals than tropical rain forests.

Temperate Rain Forests

Temperate rain forests are found in cooler regions of the world outside the tropics. New Zealand, south-eastern Australia, Tasmania, southern Chile and Argentina, Japan, and the north-west coast of North America have temperate rain forests. These forests usually grow in areas of high rainfall between mountain ranges and the ocean.

Subtropical rain forest in Lamington National Park, Queensland, Australia

There are fewer types of plants and animals in temperate rain forests compared to tropical rain forests. Sometimes temperate rain forests contain only one or two main types of tree, such as the giant sequoias of North America, which grow to more than 300 feet (90 meters) and are the most massive living things on land. The main type of tree in many temperate rain forest areas are conifers, which are also known as firs and pines.

Temperate rain forest in Olympic National Park, Washington, United States

Ecofact

Alaskan Rain Forests

The Pacific coast of North America has the largest area of temperate rain forests. They run about 1,200 miles (2,000 kilometers) along a thin coastal belt from Oregon to Alaska.

Rain Forest Layers

Tropical rain forests have four layers of life. The upper layers of the forest receive the most sunlight. The **crowns** of these trees stop most light from reaching the lower layers.

Tropical rain forest layers

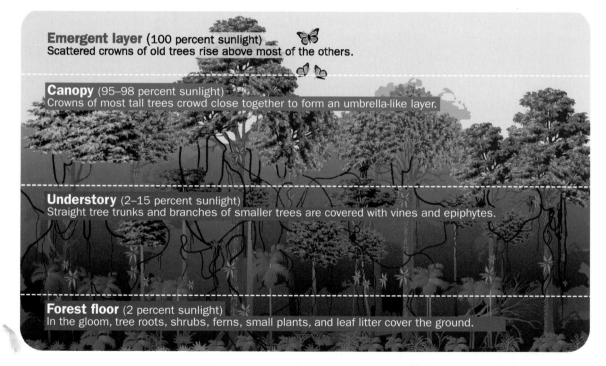

Emergent layer (100 percent sunlight)
Scattered crowns of old trees rise above most of the others.

Canopy (95–98 percent sunlight)
Crowns of most tall trees crowd close together to form an umbrella-like layer.

Understory (2–15 percent sunlight)
Straight tree trunks and branches of smaller trees are covered with vines and epiphytes.

Forest floor (2 percent sunlight)
In the gloom, tree roots, shrubs, ferns, small plants, and leaf litter cover the ground.

Ecofact

Buttress Roots

Some tropical rain forest trees have large roots that flare out from the bottom of the trunk. These can be more than 10 feet (3 meters) high and 33 feet (10 meters) long. Buttress roots help the tall trees to be stable in the thin soils.

Buttress roots, Wet Tropics World Heritage Area, Queensland, Australia

Living within the Layers

Some plants and animals live in only one layer of the forest. For example, South American capybaras, the world's largest **rodents**, live on the forest floor because they cannot climb. Other plants and animals live in more than one layer. Animals such as long-tailed macaque monkeys of southern Asia spend most of their lives in the tree layers. They rarely go down to the forest floor.

Food chains show the feeding relationship between plants and animals. A food chain starts with the Sun, water, and nutrients from the soil and **decomposing** plant and animal matter. These basic elements supply energy for plants. The next link in the chain occurs when herbivores and omnivores eat the plants. Herbivores eat only plants, while omnivores eat plants and other animals.

A food chain might continue with carnivores. These animals only eat meat. Carnivores are at the top of the food chain. When any plant or animal in the chain dies, worms and bacteria begin to decompose or break down the matter. The decomposed material returns to the soil, where plants take up the nutrients to grow, and the cycle continues.

The South American capybara lives on the forest floor.

Meat-Eating Plants

The pitcher plant, found in tropical rain forests of Southeast Asia and Australia, contains water in its pitcher which drowns insects. This carnivorous plant gets its nutrients from the decomposing insects. However, some insects, such as mosquitoes, can survive in the plant.

Pitcher plant

Emergent Layer

The tallest trees in a tropical rain forest make up the emergent layer. These forest giants may be hundreds of years old. Emergent trees grow more than 165 feet (50 meters) tall. Here and there they tower over the other treetops, which form the canopy.

At the emergent layer, winds are stronger and temperatures higher in the full sunlight. There is less humidity than the canopy below because of the strong winds.

Emergents provide lookouts for the world's largest eagles, the South American harpy eagle and the Philippine eagle, as they hunt animals in the canopy below. Most birds, monkeys, and insects, such as butterflies and moths, move between the emergent layer and the canopy looking for food. The tree tops are where most leaves, flowers, fruits, and seeds are found in tropical rain forests.

Ecofact

Butterfly Heaven

More butterflies and moths live in the emergent and canopy layers of tropical rain forests than anywhere else in the world. The largest butterfly is the poisonous Queen Alexandra's Birdwing, from Papua New Guinea. It is almost 11 inches (28 centimeters) across. The largest moth in the world is the Hercules or atlas moth, from the rain forests of Australia and New Guinea. It is up to 10 inches (25 centimeters) across.

A young harpy eagle sits on its nest in the emergent layer of the rain forest in Peru.

Emergent Layer Food Chain

Even in the tallest trees in the rain forest, there are many plants and animals connected in food chains. Here is an example of a food chain from the emergent layer in an African tropical rain forest.

Emergent tree gets its energy from the Sun, and nutrients from soil and decaying matter on the forest floor.

1 →

Insects and caterpillars (herbivores) eat the leaves of the emergent tree.

2

6 Emergent tree takes up soil nutrients.

5 Crowned eagle dies and falls to the forest floor, where it is broken down by worms and bacteria (decomposers). The nutrients are returned to the soil.

Emergent layer food chain

3

Kirk's red colobus monkey (omnivore) eats insects, caterpillars, and leaves.

4

A crowned eagle (carnivore), sometimes called a crowned hawk eagle, eats the colobus monkey.

13

Canopy

The canopy is the rain forest's main layer. The crowns of trees form an umbrella-like covering ranging from 65 to 165 feet (20 to 50 meters) above the ground. The canopy has many epiphytes growing on the trunks and branches of trees. They get their nutrients from the rain and air.

The canopy and the understory are home to more than 70 percent of all rain forest plants and animals. These include birds, mammals, marsupials, reptiles, spiders, and insects. The blossom bat of New Guinea is a nocturnal animal that **pollinates** many tropical rain forest trees. It never leaves the canopy layer. Many other animals rarely leave this layer. They find food, water, and shelter within the tree tops.

Ecofact

Climbing Kangaroos

Tree kangaroos are the "monkeys" of tropical rain forests in Australia and New Guinea. Their sharp claws help them to climb easily, and their long tail helps them balance as they leap up to 23 feet (7 meters) between trees.

Tree kangaroo in the canopy of a New Guinea rain forest

Life in the Canopy

Some animals and plants have **adaptations** to help them survive in different environments. In a tropical rain forest canopy, some monkeys, such as the spider monkey, have **prehensile** tails. Their tails wrap around branches like a fifth limb and help them to reach food. Gliding geckos have special webbed feet and flaps of skin on their sides to help them to glide from tree to tree. Paradise tree snakes are able to flatten their bodies and glide between trees.

Many tropical rain forest trees, such as figs, have strong-smelling flowers and fleshy, colored fruit, which attract animals. Animals such as sugar gliders and possums pollinate the flowers, while hornbills and fruit bats eat the fruit and spread the seeds. These plants need the animals in order to reproduce, and the animals need the plants for food. Scientists call this **interdependence**.

Ecofact

World of Birds

The canopy and emergent layers of tropical rain forests have 30 percent of the world's birds. These range from giant eagles weighing 17 pounds (8 kilograms), to tiny hummingbirds weighing only a few ounces (grams). Rain forests have more types of parrots than any other type of ecosystem.

A South American macaw parrot

An Australian fruit bat

Understory

In a tropical rain forest, the canopy allows about 2 to 15 percent of light to reach the layer below. The air in the understory is hot, still, and humid. The plants are adapted to shade. They include tree ferns, palms, smaller trees, epiphytes, and shrubs. Climbing palms called rattans and vines called lianas use hooks and spiky thorns to climb from the forest floor to the understory, and then upwards to the canopy.

Many **saplings** of canopy trees grow slowly here, waiting for a break in the canopy. When a tree falls, sunlight finally reaches the understory. Then there is a race by the younger trees to fill the gap in the canopy.

Birds, insects, frogs, lizards, and snakes, such as green tree pythons and yellow tree boas, are common. Cats, such as leopards, jaguars, jaguarundi, and ocelots, hunt in the understory.

An ocelot in a rain forest understory in Venezuela, South America

Animal Adaptations

Tropical rain forest animals in the darker understory have also made many adaptations to help them survive. Some iguanas, chameleons, snakes, and cats use **camouflage** to hide from predators or their prey. The giant stick insect and the Asian leaf frog imitate plants. By looking like a plant, they can avoid being eaten. Tree pangolins have scaly armor to protect themselves from **predators**.

Poison-arrow frogs carry their tiny tadpoles around on their backs. They look for pools of water in bromeliads, which are epiphytes related to the pineapple family. The tadpoles are put into the bromeliad pond and their mother visits them daily until they change into frogs. They live their entire life cycle in the understory.

Chameleons are tree lizards whose skin helps them to blend in with their surroundings.

Forest Floor

About 2 percent of light reaches the tropical rain forest floor. Plants such as mosses, **lichens**, and ferns grow slowly. Fallen leaves and branches litter the ground. Insects, worms, fungi, and bacteria quickly decompose the dead matter and put nutrients back in the soil. Plants then take up nutrients, such as calcium and nitrogen, and store them.

The largest animals in the tropical rain forest also live on the forest floor. African rain forests have gorillas, forest elephants, and **okapi**, which are related to giraffes. Southeast Asian forests have Sumatran rhinoceroses, Asian elephants, and tigers. South American forests have capybaras, which are like giant guinea pigs, and peccaries, which are related to pigs. Tapirs live in Southeast Asia and South America. They are related to rhinoceroses and horses, and are good swimmers.

A tiger in a Asian rain forest

Forest Floor Food Chain

Even in the gloom of the rain forest floor, many plants and animals are connected in food chains. Here is an example of a food chain from the forest floor in a South American tropical rain forest.

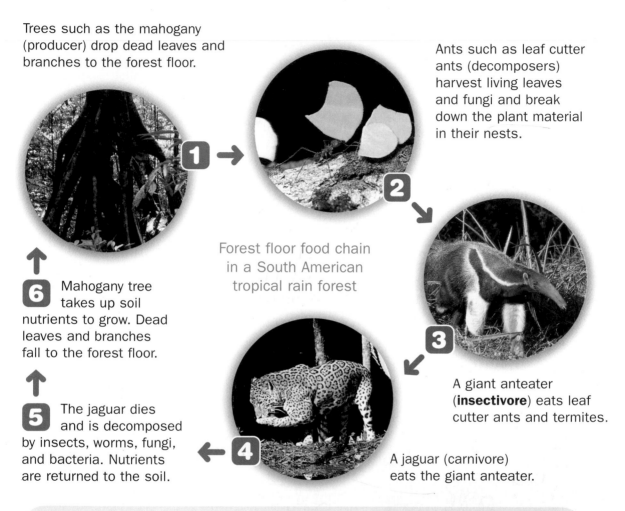

Trees such as the mahogany (producer) drop dead leaves and branches to the forest floor.

Ants such as leaf cutter ants (decomposers) harvest living leaves and fungi and break down the plant material in their nests.

Forest floor food chain in a South American tropical rain forest

6 Mahogany tree takes up soil nutrients to grow. Dead leaves and branches fall to the forest floor.

5 The jaguar dies and is decomposed by insects, worms, fungi, and bacteria. Nutrients are returned to the soil.

A giant anteater (**insectivore**) eats leaf cutter ants and termites.

A jaguar (carnivore) eats the giant anteater.

Ecofact

World's Largest Flower

Rafflesia is a **parasitic plant** from Southeast Asia that grows on a host vine on the forest floor. It has no leaves but grows up to 3 feet (91 centimeters) across and weighs up to 24 pounds (11 kilograms). The plant smells like rotting meat, and this attracts insects, such as flies, which pollinate the flower.

A rafflesia plant on the forest floor in Malaysia

Indigenous Peoples

About 1,000 groups of indigenous peoples have lived in tropical rain forests for thousands of years. They gather plant foods and hunt wild animals and fish. Some groups also plant crops, such as yams and bananas, in clearings they make in the forest. They move their gardens every few years when the soil loses nutrients. This is called shifting agriculture, or slash-and-burn farming.

A Penan man hunts by shooting poisoned darts through a blowpipe in Sarawak, Malaysia.

Peoples of the tropical rain forest

Region	Indigenous Peoples	States/Countries Where They Live Today
Africa	Bambuti pygmies	Democratic Republic of Congo, Cameroon, Congo
Asia	Penan	Sarawak, Malaysia
Australia	Aboriginal peoples	Australia
Pacific Islands	Melanesian peoples	Papua New Guinea, Solomon Islands, Vanuatu
South America	Yanomami	Brazil, Venezuela

Indigenous Knowledge and Adaptations

Indigenous peoples have a great knowledge of the tropical rain forest. They know which plants and animals are good to eat, which to use as medicines and which are poisonous. They know how to use the poisons from some plants and animals for hunting and fishing. They also know how to look after the rain forest.

Rain forest people have adapted to their environment. They sweat less and drink less water than other people because their food has a lot of water in it. They are usually shorter than the average person. The Mbuti pygmies of Africa are the world's smallest people. They are under 5 feet (1.5 meters) in height.

Ecofact

Yanomami People

There are 20,000 Yanomami living in Brazil and Venezuela. In 1985, outsiders discovered gold in the Yanomami territory. The miners brought diseases that many of the Yanomami people could not fight off. Today, governments have protected the rights of these people and made reserves for them.

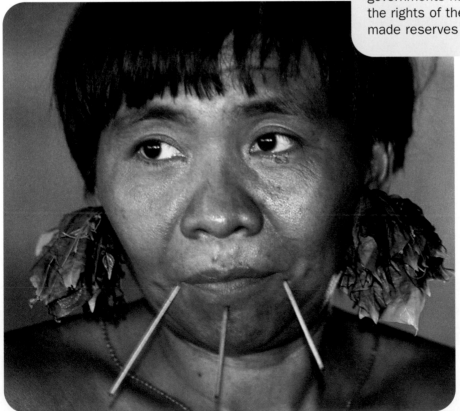

A Yanomami woman

Rain Forest Resources

Tropical rain forests supply many valuable things for people. Hardwood timber, such as mahogany, ebony, and teak, grows in rain forests and is used for furniture and building. Many tropical rain forests are being cleared faster than trees can regrow. Without planning and protection, rain forest resources, such as timber, will not last forever.

Valuable Crops from Rain Forests

Many valuable crops came from tropical rain forests. Some wild crops, such as Brazil nuts and rubber from South America, and durians from southern Asia, are still harvested from rain forests. Most of the other crops are now grown on farms in areas with a rain forest climate.

New varieties of useful plants are still being discovered in tropical rain forests. In Papua New Guinea, there are 251 types of rain forest trees that produce edible fruit. People are growing only 43 of these.

Useful crops from rain forests around the world

Region	Crops
Africa	coffee, palm oil, cola
Asia and Australasia	pepper, ginger, jackfruit, lychee, rambutan, mango, macadamia, sugar cane, bananas, plantain, yam, taro, winged bean, nutmeg, mace
Central and South America	cashew nuts, pineapple, tree tomato, vanilla, avocadoes, cocoa, cassava

Wild Avocado Trees

There are around 85 types of wild avocado trees in Central America. Some are resistant to diseases. Scientists crossbreed these with the types farmers grow in tropical and subtropical areas. This helps farmers to produce better avocado crops.

Avocadoes are delicious rain forest fruits.

Nature's Medicine Chest

Tropical rain forest plants supply chemicals for 25 percent of the world's prescription drugs. At least 70 percent of the plants used to fight cancer come from tropical rain forests. The rosy periwinkle from Madagascar produces chemicals used to treat a cancer of the blood called leukemia. Quinine is a drug used to treat malaria. It comes from the bark of the South American cinchona tree.

Indigenous peoples use thousands of rain forest plants as medicines. There are many undiscovered medicines in tropical rain forests. If tropical rain forests are cleared for timber, farming, and ranching, future sources of medicines and crops will be lost forever.

The rosy periwinkle, from Madagascar, is used to treat cancer.

Ecofact

Chemical Prospecting

Chemical prospecting is the process of looking for useful chemicals in living organisms. Some drug companies pay a fee to the government of a country to search for useful organisms in their rain forests. This helps the government earn money without damaging the rain forests.

Threats to Rain Forests

There are many threats to rain forests, including fires, wars, and the building of roads, industries, cities, mines, and dams. However, the biggest threat to rain forests is clearing. Worldwide, about 42 million acres (17 million hectares) of tropical rain forest are cleared each year. The trees are used for firewood and timber, or just burned. Cleared land is mainly used for grazing beef cattle and growing crops.

Many poor countries with tropical rain forests are under pressure to make land available to their growing populations for farming and ranching. Poor countries also owe other rich countries lots of money. Some of the money from logging tropical rain forests and farming and ranching the cleared land is used to pay back the rich countries. However, the poor soils are not good for growing crops and the land is not very productive. The cleared land makes very little money. Once rain forests are cleared, the **habitat** for the rain forest plants and animals is gone forever.

Ecofact

Rain Forest Clearing

Almost half of the world's rain forests have disappeared over the past 50 years. About 10 percent of the Amazon's forests have been cleared, mainly for farming and grazing cattle. Small and large farmers, local and international companies, and governments are involved in clearing rain forests.

Clearing rain forest in Belize, Central America

Endangered Plants and Animals

Because people are destroying rain forests, many rain forest plants and animals are endangered. These plants and animals can only live in rain forests. If their habitat disappears, they will become extinct. Humans who hunt or trade endangered plants and animals push them to extinction faster.

Scientists believe some tropical rain forest plants and animals have already become extinct. Eight types of macaw are extinct in Central America. There are only a few hundred mountain gorillas left in Africa. Indonesia has the highest number of endangered parrots. One of the world's rarest monkeys, the golden lion tamarin, lives in one small reserve in Brazil, South America. There are only about 500 wild animals left, and the reserve is sometimes threatened by fire. The problem of endangered rain forest plants and animals can be solved if enough rain forests are protected.

Ecofact

The Endangered Island

Madagascar is a large island off the east coast of Africa. Almost 70 percent of its rain forests have been cleared for farming. The island has 160,000 unique plants and animals, including 29 types of lemur. The rarest lemur is the aye-aye, a **nocturnal** insectivore. Many of the island's plants and animals are endangered because their habitat is disappearing.

Lemurs from Madagascar

The African mountain gorilla is threatened with extinction.

Effects of Clearing Rain Forests

Rain forests act like a giant sponge and help to control flooding. They also protect soils from being washed away. When the forests are cleared, flooding and soil erosion become problems.

Tropical rain forests are called "the lungs of the world." They help control the world's climate by absorbing large amounts of carbon dioxide and releasing large amounts of oxygen. The trees store carbon to help prevent global warming.

Clearing and burning rain forest leaves the land prone to flooding and erosion.

Endangered Peoples

There were about 10 to 15 million indigenous people in the Amazon Basin some 500 years ago. Many were killed by settlers or died from diseases that these people brought with them. Today, there are about one million indigenous Amazonian people in 500 groups. Some are threatened because the rain forests where they live are being cleared.

When tropical rain forests are cleared, the climate of the whole planet is affected. Rainfall patterns change. When trees are burned, carbon dioxide is released. This adds to global warming. As a result, sea levels rise and some coastal areas may be flooded. Many millions of people around the world may lose their homes if this continues.

Indigenous people also lose their homes and their way of life when the forests are cleared. Their great knowledge of the forest is also lost.

Ecotourism in Rain Forests

Ecotourism is when visitors pay to see the beauty of a natural ecosystem. People want to visit tropical rain forests because they are the world's richest ecosystem. Ecotourism does not cause much disturbance to the rain forests. In many areas, governments and local people can earn more money from people visiting rain forests than from clearing them.

Ecotourism is the largest industry in Costa Rica. It is also growing in importance in many other countries with tropical rain forests. Indigenous people can become guides, showing visitors rain forest plants and animals. Ecotourism can help protect some valuable rain forest areas for the future.

Ecotourism helps to protect this black howler monkey's rain forest home from being cleared.

Ecofact

Ecotourism in Belize

A reserve for black howler monkeys around farmland in Belize, Central America, attracts 6,000 tourists a year. Local farmers act as tour guides and provide food and lodging for the tourists. The farmers and the monkeys benefit by keeping the rain forest alive.

Protecting Rain Forests

More laws are needed to prevent rain forests from being destroyed. At present, only 6 percent of the world's rain forests are protected in national parks and reserves. Less than 4 percent of Africa's rain forests are protected.

Governments need to do more to save the most important rain forest areas before it is too late. Scientists say that at least 10 percent of rain forests need to be protected in parks and reserves so that most of their plant and animal species can survive. These parks also need to be large enough to allow that.

Some rich countries have helped poor countries like Costa Rica and Ecuador to create reserves. People and governments around the world need to be aware of the threats to rain forests and take action to preserve what is left.

A rain forest reserve in Ecuador

Ecofact

Costa Rica

National parks protect 12 percent of the tiny country of Costa Rica. Ecotourism is an important way of earning money for the country. There are also special reserves in the national parks for indigenous peoples.

Conservation Groups

International conservation groups such as the World Wildlife Fund (WWF) also help protect rain forests. They let many people know about the problems faced by rain forests. In the west African country of Cameroon, WWF has worked with the local people in Korup National Park to save the tropical rain forests from clearing and hunting. WWF helped the people to learn crafts, such as basket weaving, so they can make a living from the forests.

Some conservation groups buy land for rain forest reserves. They organize scientists to investigate and write reports on the value of rain forest areas. Conservation groups also pressure governments to set up reserves and pass laws to protect endangered plants and animals. Through the efforts of these groups, international agreements have been made to stop the illegal trade in endangered animals.

Greenpeace activists protest against the logging of the Amazon rainforest.

How to Save Rain Forests

We can all work to save rain forests. You can learn more about the importance of rain forests to the world. Join a conservation group and let others know about the threats to rain forests. Do not buy items made from harvested rain forest woods. Write to the government and ask them to help save the world's rain forests. The governments of rich countries can help poor countries protect their rain forests for the good of everyone.

ecosystems

The following web sites give more information on rain forests.

Dr Blythe's rain forest education
http://www.rainforesteducation.com/

Forests
http://www.ucmp.berkeley.edu/glossary/gloss5/biome/forests.html

Rain forests
http://curriculum.calstatela.edu/courses/builders/lessons/less/biomes/rainforest/rainintro.html

Rain forests
http://mbgnet.mobot.org/sets/rforest/

The rain forest biome
http://oncampus.richmond.edu/academics/as/education/projects/webunits/biomes/rainforest.html

Virtual rain forest
http://www.msu.edu/~urquhar5/tour/active.html

Zoom rain forests
http://www.enchantedlearning.com/subjects/rainforest

Glossary

adaptations	changes that help plants and animals survive in an environment
camouflage	when an animal's color or shape help it to blend into the background
cloud forests	rain forests found above 10,000 feet (3,000 meters)
crowns	the top branches and leaves of trees
decomposing	breaking down
habitat	the environment where organisms live
highland rain forests	rain forests found above 3,300 feet (1,000 meters)
indigenous peoples	groups of people who first lived in a place, whose traditional ways help them to survive in that place
insectivore	an animal that eats insects
interdependence	when plants and animals depend upon each other for survival
lichens	plants that grow over surfaces, such as rocks and trees
lowland rain forests	rain forests found below 3,300 feet (1,000 meters)
nocturnal	animals that come out at night to feed
nutrients	minerals and chemicals in the soil
okapi	an African rain forest antelope related to the giraffe
parasitic plant	a plant that feeds off another plant
pollinates	when insects, birds, or animals fertilize the flower of a plant
predators	animals that hunt and eat other animals
prehensile	adapted to grasping by wrapping around
primates	a group of mammals that includes humans, apes, monkeys, and lemurs
rodents	small mammals with sharp front teeth
saplings	young trees
species	types of plants and animals
unique	one of a kind

Index